Arvind Krishna Mehrotra

Of Least Concern

Arvind Krishna Mehrotra

Of Least Concern

Shearsman Books

Published in the United Kingdom in 2025 by
Shearsman Books Ltd
PO Box 4239
Swindon   SN3 9FN

Shearsman Books Ltd Registered Office
30–31 St. James Place, Mangotsfield, Bristol BS16 9JB
(this address not for correspondence)

EU AUTHORISED REPRESENTATIVE:
Lightning Source France, 1 Av. Johannes Gutenberg,
78310 Maurepas, France
Email: compliance@lightningsource.fr

www.shearsman.com

ISBN 978-1-84861-989-0

ACKNOWLEDGEMENTS

Grateful acknowledgement is made to the editors of the following
journals and anthologies where some of these poems first appeared:
Almost Island, At the Louvre (ed. Louvre Museum, New York Review
Books, 2024), *Down to Earth, Harvard Review, Hazel Press Blog, Indian
Express, Literary Activism, Open, Poetry* (Chicago), *Poetry and Covid-19*
(eds. Anthony Caleshu and Rory Waterman, Shearsman Books, 2021),
Poetry London, Reliquiae, South Parade, The Common, and *The Punch
Magazine.*

'Resting Places' and 'Small Holdings' were first published in limited
editions by Longhouse. My thanks to Bob and Susan Arnold.

The description of the white-eye's nest in 'Lockdown Garden 19' is taken
from Salim Ali's much-reprinted classic *The Book of Indian Birds* (OUP).

But God hath chosen the foolish things of the world to confound the wise; and God had chosen the weak things of the world to confound the things which are mighty; And base things of the world, and things which are despised, hath God chosen, *yea*, and things which are not, to bring to nought things that are.

(1 Corinthians 1: 27-8)

Contents

Author's Note   10

I. Lockdown Garden   13

II. Lakeside Walks   35

III. Five Letters   43

IV. Resting Places   51

V. A Matter of Facts

Before the New Day   73
Asleep in a Crib   74
Solstice   75
Brick Kiln   76
Rishikesh   77
Jay Walker   78
A Matter of Facts   79
Sparrow Population   81
New Turmeric Leaf   83
Torso   84
Three or Four Squirrels,
     Two Bulbuls, One Magpie-Robin   85
No Sooner had the Rain   86
Ants   87
Avenue Tree in Private Garden   88
Parasite   89
Hack   90

Fire Wall   91
Registry of Births,
        Deaths and Marriages   92
Possibly Theban   94
Cremation at Nalapani Road   95
Approaching 80   96
Nothing Worked Out   97
We'll Never Know the Names   98
House of Peeling Walls   99
Like a Stone   100
Aubade   101

VI. Small Holdings   103

For Amit and Rinka

Author's Note

The first six poems in this book, "Lockdown Garden 1-6", were written soon after the first Covid lockdown was declared on March 24, 2020. The weather was mild and the roads, except for patrol cars, deserted. There was a hush in the air and a padlock on the gate. Forced to stay at home, there was in me a new watchfulness.

The house in which I live, once called Anne Villa, was built around 1900 and belonged to the Lumsdens. Mr. Lumsden was in the furniture business. After he died, his wife and children returned to Scotland. My paternal grandfather, Ram Prasad, a civil engineer from Thomason College, Roorkee, bought the house in 1926 from the Allahabad Bank, which held the mortgage. It is this house to which my mother brought me in 1947, weeks after my birth in Lahore. An inherited house is like a parent that outlives the parents. During Covid I began to see, in the shingled paths around it, what had always lain unnoticed under my feet.

Except 'Lakeside Walks', almost everything else in these pages lies within the straight walls of an irregularly laid out garden, much reduced from what it was originally. The garden, such shape as it now has, was not given it by design. It came about through indifference. There is the semblance of a lawn. Bald in patches and weedy, it is bordered on three sides by mango and litchi trees. Two Chinese fan palms stand in one corner. Between the trees are crotons, aloe vera, bloodleaves, spider lilies, mondo grass, a shrub called yesterday-today-tomorrow, and – pulled out from a roadside ditch – a plant whose name I've still to find out. The trees were planted so close to each other that not only did they stunt each other's growth, they killed what lawn there was. No thought was given to what went where. Unplanned, everything in the garden choked everything else, while allowing everything to flourish. This morning the self-seeded bitter melon was putting forth new tendrils to support itself on the self-seeded pink periwinkle. There's also a back garden, where the large trees are – the cluster fig, the flame of the forest, the teak, the camphor, the neem, the dillenia, the coral, the Java plum, and still more mango and litchi trees. The slow-growing Ceylon ironwood doesn't mix with its neighbours. The drumstick has had an unfortunate life. The mulberry has constantly to be brought down to earth. The peach and lemon trees seem entangled with each other. Without realising it, I'd been trying to grow an old contiguous forest quickly. At its edges is a human settlement.

Throughout the first lockdown, which lasted for nine weeks, I would, at around 7 every morning, take out a red folding chair and sit under the peach. I would open my spiral notebook and, pencil in hand, begin to "draw". I, who can only make stick figures, drew as might an artist working outdoors. Anyone observing me from across the wall would surely think so. Every now and then I'd look up vacantly to check if what I was absorbed in making bore any resemblance to the scene in front of me, or to the one in my mind, the latter, as yet, not entirely visible. I was, in these moments, searching for a word that would strike me months later. Perhaps the nearest description of what I was doing is a passage in Coleridge's *Biographia Literaria*: "With my pencil and memorandum book in my hand, I was making studies, as the artists call them, and often moulding my thoughts into verse, with the objects and imagery immediately before my senses."

It was the same garden that I stepped into day after day – at 7 am, at 7 pm, and at all times in between and before and after – but you cannot step into the same garden twice. There is, to this, a corollary (a word whose etymology has, happily, to do with flowers): once you step into a garden you cannot step out of it. A sunbird approaches the trumpet vine or a leaf falls and, once again, you begin to follow a trail of thought that may or may not have anything to do with what is before you. The Covid epidemic had come and gone but the stick figures I drew acquired leaves and wings and tails and petals. They began to crawl and fly and make nests. My notebooks filled up with more and more drawings, now gathered in this book. It's been a see-saw. At times I felt was I a mere copyist. At others the opposite was true: had I stopped seeing the "imagery immediately before my senses"?

Whatever else it may be, a book of poems is also a municipal registry of births, marriages and deaths. This book is no exception.

June 28, 2024   16 Old Survey Road
                                                            Dehradun

I

LOCKDOWN GARDEN

The Master said: "Little Ones, why don't you study the *Poems*? … Also, you will learn there the names of many birds, animals, plants, and trees."

Confucius, *Analects* 17.9 tr. Simon Leys

1

Close to each other,
socially undistanced,
the mulberry leaves,

uniformly green,
shall turn brown together.
It's like a herd dying.

2

Firm to begin with,
the mud clod
could've injured you.
It crumbles in your hand.

3

In the heap of dead
leaves crinkly as
brown skins, those
breathing things
foraging around
the bamboo stand
are jungle babblers.

4

It was planted
all wrong, too
close to a wall,
under the mango
trees. There was
nowhere for it
to go except up
like a mast and
that's where
it went, taking
its leaves with it –
long, tapering.
I never saw them
fall. It never
flowered, which
would've helped
me look it up in a
book of flowering
Indian trees. Now
I'll never know
its name nor of
the bird singing
at evening
in the shrubbery.

5

She stood outside
the gate, a woman
my age, head covered
with flowery print,
a sickle in her hand.

Could she come
inside and cut
grass for her goats?
It was ankle high.
Her face was inches

from mine and I felt
her breath on my skin.
It's after I'd turned
the corner that I heard
what she'd said.

6

The shingles unwalked on,
the doors bolted,
the squirrels back in their nests.

Under the moon a bird floats
and settles on a branch.
The sky is pale.

The leaves of the ironwood
when new every spring
are a deep pink.

The evening goes out like a flame.
We've seen different things.
It's always been so.

Tell me, love, what you saw today?

7
The bats came in low
and circled the litchi trees
at three in the morning.

I couldn't see how many there were,
unless there was only one
and the others its winged shadows

more black than the night I stood in.

8
The garden, unlike you,
is a daytime presence. I wait
for this night to be over,
for the trees to reappear
in window and doorway.

9

Its root hairs fair
as cheek down,
its weedy flower
like a pinch of
cotton wool pressed
against a vein,
I hold the uprooted
plant in my hand.
It grew on the ledge,
on a patch of moss.

10

Because you said the young
leaves of the bitter neem are
sweet, I went looking
for them to the bottom
of the garden and found

the tree's lowest branch too high
to reach. Returning by a less
familiar route, I stubbed my toe
on a brickbat camouflaged in
sour-leafed wood sorrel.

11
The willow
that poured leaves in spring,
is overrun by king's mantle
and dry as stone.

12
Watered,
the bloodleaves lose
their droop and glow
in the western sun

under the litchi,
that in April
is covered in blossom,
in May with parrots.

13
The milk thistle's
bud I saw
in the pink of health

is a white smudge,
like a child's drawing
rubbed with spittle.

14
The bark is smooth, flaky,
the trunk hollow;
midway, black-edged, is a hole
big enough to put your hand in
or the whole arm. From two
sides, branches come out, whip-
thin, green-tipped. The tree
is otherwise bare. Too tall to be
a stump, the crepe myrtle
is preparing to flower.

15

Three new basil plants
have sprung up this monsoon,
each three feet apart,

as though the wind
had measured the distance
before dispersing the seeds.

16

As I came up with the morning papers,
the pigeon walking on the balustrade
flew off to join two squirrels

under the plumeria,
leaving me alone to scan the day's headlines
which I'd read the previous week.

17

The kill in its beak,
the Himalayan bulbul
thrashes its head
from side to side.

Only the butterfly's
blue wings are found
amidst the dead leaves
and pine needles.

18

Planted as groundcover,
the arrowhead vine mass produces
arrowhead leaves in season
and out, whether you notice or not.

Thus a civilian garden
gets militarised, not that the military
lacks gardens of its own to grow,
in wartime and peace, prize dahlias.

19

The nest
"slung hammockwise
in the end fork
of a thin twig";

the eggs pale blue;
domestic duties
shared equally:

all this the white-eye
said as it turned
to look at me
through the leaves.

20

Its guavas inedible
and the trunk a broken stick
on which it leans, it holds fast

to its one branch
as I do to my father
who planted the sapling,
his photograph fading on the wall
along with the Fifties hairstyle.

21
The white butterfly
folded its papery wings

and disappeared into the tiger's claw,
its flight unsteady when it left.

22
I heard a sound,
saw something fall.
What I saw was not
the sound I heard.

The sound I heard
was a mango falling.
What I saw
was a falling leaf.

23
The last time I saw you
there were dandelions
growing in the lawn.

The years gone by
seem shorter
than the few to come.

24

A stone that none saw coming
smashed the drumstick's head.
It was four months old.

I went back for a replacement
and was given the same instructions
I'd been given before:

"Use a razor blade and make three cuts
 in the plastic – here, here, and here.
When you lower the plant into the pit

make sure the soil is intact.
Water it on alternate days,
and always away from the roots.

We've said a prayer for it
at home. We do it for all our saplings.
It'll thrive."

25

They're the garden's
industrial workers,
its hard hats.

But what is the pink
rain lily doing
among the marigolds?

26
The amaranth has gone to seed.
The silk oak drops a flower.
A squirrel chases a butterfly,
the butterfly runs circles round the squirrel.
Passing a bush, I pick curry leaves to chew.

The house I stepped out of is the shore I left.
The garden I'm adrift in has ripples like the sea.

27
There's no pattern to it.
Trees go sideways or straight;
one has a curved trunk.
In the flowerbed is aloe vera.

Anything grows anywhere
in this garden, when you notice
through the porte-cochère's pointed arch
the rubber plant's pointed leaf.

28
Set with raindrops, displayed
between the king's mantle and the litchi tree,
was the cobweb I almost walked into.

After an hour, when I returned,
the light had changed, the raindrops
were smaller, the glitter had gone,

and there was no sign of the occupant.

29
A danger to the house
and too big to cut down,
the silk oak when it falls
will be a ship sinking.

30
When a branch
of the dillenia fell

it was as if a corrugated sheet
had been ripped off the tree.

Behind it, above the garden shed,
rose a blue hill in the distance.

31
Left untrained,
the bitter melon's taken over
the mulberry, dusting it

with small yellow flowers.
The females will shrivel,
then elongate with the goodness

of bitterness. The males
will drop by the wayside
no sooner than they're touched.

Had they wings,
they'd have turned
into butterflies and joined

the fantail-flycatcher
making figures of eight
at the other end of the garden.

32

Crushed by the cluster fig's lopped branch,
the hophead Philippine violet didn't recover.
But in an unvisited corner of the garden where the
        marijuana's
invasive and dead wood rots, a new one's come up.
It's still young with flexible spikes,
and already looks to escape
from hazardous garden to safe bushland.

33

Spotted with rust,
the leaves had fallen,
the holes in them like blown
windows in a war zone.

When I planted it,
no astrologer told me
that the teak would not live
to see its third year.

I watered it in summer
and saw it grow,
comparing its height
to mine as I passed.

34
A change of location
from veranda to terrace,
a tumbler or two of water,
and the curled leaf
of the potted lime opens.

His face covered with
pellet marks, the Srinagar
schoolboy opened his eyes.
"The light hurts," he said.
"Turn it off."

35
I pulled up a chair to sit
by the Rangoon creeper.
It had been cut back
and was spreading again
through the balusters.

Just then I heard
Caw! Caw!
It came from a house
in a twice-erased city
where after the coal fire

had been put out
and the cook had left,
when crows were thick on the ground
and everyone was asleep,
I'd watch through a window crack

dark-skinned fairies
wearing yellow oleander
flowers in their hair, bathing
under custard apple trees
on summer afternoons.

36

Seeing that the green stem
projecting over the low brick wall
had entered his air space,

he broke it in two and left it
dangling on the branch
to teach me a lesson.

37

Around this time every evening
I'm out in the garden looking for things to pick.
The drumstick has again lost half its height
and the dillenia is fast losing its leaves.
The ironwood is white with flowers.
Yesterday, when it was getting dark,
I saw something lying near it.
It looked like a petal. It's getting dark again.
The dillenia's leafless, the ironwood's flowering,
and my basket is heavy with leaves, petals, and dusk.

38

It's seven in the evening.

There are no clothes
on the clothesline
on which two bulbuls sit

for just long enough
to show their silhouettes.
A squirrel disappears
behind the meat safe

as another heads for
the camphor tree.
They may not say so,
but they have things to do.

39
The day is joyous.
Green string lights on trees.
Each leaf's covered
and no leaf's fused.

There's a Zoom wedding on
and you're in bridal dress.
Its flight reflected in a puddle,
a bird passes overhead.

40
Our house is the forest floor:

wood-panelled walls, a dead willow
with bracket fungi, empty shelves.

The place is ready,
waiting for our stuff
to arrive.

41
There are no greaters or lessers left.

There's nothing left to classify,
nothing to multiply either.

The last coucal pair
was spotted in two gardens
separated by five degrees of latitude.

42

The sky black with clouds,

eight weeks into the rains,
there is in the garden
something white unfurling.

Loose of limb, a strappy body,
it has all the parts
of a spider lily: hands, feet, skin,
and black-rimmed eyes.

43

Was it your spoken
or your written voice I heard
as I bent to see where
the dumb nettle had
disappeared in the oxeyes?
Can you say it again?

44

The blue wishbone flower
I saw on the walk
was found growing under the mango tree
in the garden.

I hadn't noticed it before
though it must've been there,
and will be there again, if the tree is there,
this time next year.

45

It's quiet on Sunday afternoons,
a time to watch pigeons walking across
the street as though they were crossing

the sky. The mango trees bordering the lawn
were planted the year psephology
came to India, but the golden rain sapling

planted last month is catching up,
putting out new leaves
the colour of buried copper.

46

Behind the untrimmed croton,
perfectly shaped, covered
with violet, lilac, and white
flowers whose fragrance
you can smell as you go past,
is yesterday-today-tomorrow.
But today the small butterflies
that flash by in broad daylight.

II

LAKESIDE WALKS

1

This lakeside,
this Inner Mongolia,
where the language spoken
is the one you speak

to yourself when you see,
after a rain shower,
a droplet on a leaf tip
or a snail on its way to somewhere.

2

Every few days
walking under trees
I raise an arm to touch a leaf.

You're slightly
out of reach.

3

By the time we came
it was too late, but this
we knew before we came:

we weren't untouched
by wind and rain, weren't quite
the squirrels in the grass

chasing the other's tail.
The old rain makes the new ground muddy
and we cannot see with this wind in our eyes.

4

A man who looks like a stuffed toy
is sitting at a picnic table. He does not move.
There's an unlit cigarette in his hand.

Across from him is a four-lane highway and a walking path
on which hollow bricks have been dumped to make a wall.
The government does as it likes. It has nothing to hide.

It's been a while since I saw a mongoose.
Recently, she wrote to say that she saw one and mistook it
        for a cat.
It was big. We write to each other every day.

There's a storm brewing.
The man who looked like a stuffed toy
may not survive

but if I see him again I'll read his thoughts.
Deaths and memories come in no order.
My thoughts he can read here.

5

"There's always room at the top," said my grandfather when
I ran into him in Washington Square Park. He was eating an
ice cream.
It was a hot day.
"Scum rises to the top fastest," said the landlady to a cousin
doing his articles in London.
The cyclist made as if to kick the street dog giving chase,
stopping it in its tracks.

A young man, no shoes, walks about aimlessly, which is
the same as purposefully.
A fallen branch blocks the way. I'm forced to step over it.
Love's a form of verse as much as a sonnet, and so long
as there are bushes, ragpickers will never be short of rags
to pick.

6

It was raining when I left.
By the time I reached the sun was out.
Where the sun fell the cobbles were dry.
I walked on the dry patches. A man in a reflective jacket
swept the leaves. Yesterday, I'd passed a piebald cow.
It was dead. It wasn't there today.
I passed four dogs. When I saw them again, one of them
lifted its leg at the front wheel of my car.
There was no need to tell you any of this.
Of that which there's no need to tell
is sometimes the most telling.

7

Short black hair, brown with dust;
leather slip-ons; green flares;
a white shirt that's turned grey, bright ribbons pinned on it;
tied round her head a piece of cloth,
its ends reaching her waist.
She stood before a tree, tapping a plastic bottle,
listening to the music she made.

8

Behind a tree guard of cast-iron lace,
a five-petalled flower of dark pink
with a black centre;

in a brass inkpot on a chest of drawers,
a pinwheel bought
at a fair.

Between the long toes of buttress roots
I saw it growing, the pinwheel flower
that kept spinning

even when there was no wind.

9

Light shines
through grey clouds;
a eucalyptus,

like arms raised in praise or prayer,
spreads its branches upwards;
small yellow butterflies

flying close to each other
make it hard to tell
if they're two or one.

10
I walked for thirty
minutes today;
no, twenty-eight.
Not that it makes
a difference.
Two minutes.

The plant I thought
was roadside greenery
had two flowers: small,
bluish, with a yellow
throat. I have
sent you the pic on
WhatsApp. See if

you can identify it.

11
A poem like a tree
can be dated precisely.

For instance, today
I saw a blue
face mask hanging
on a branch.

12

Two mynas, eyes right,
goose-stepping on flagstones.

They'll be around when the goose-steppers
are gone like a drying patch

of rain water
on a park bench.

III

FIVE LETTERS

1

The bricklayer was here, rebuilding
the wall that had fallen in the storm.
He'd knock off the old mortar,
settle the brick into position,
then reach for the next one,
his eye precise as a mason line.
These bricks are perfectly good.
We don't need more.
If he saw a scorpion scuttling about
he waited for it to get away.
I once had a singing bricklayer.
This one was talkative.
Finished for the day, he sat
by the garden tap and washed
his implements, his hands and feet
before looking at the wall,
then at me. *It lets in air and light*, he said.
appreciatively. It also saves on bricks.
I was a willing apprentice.
The pierced brick design was his idea.

2

The grey of the sky
that had settled like an iron
lid on the green
of mulberry, peach, litchi,
camphor, and cluster fig,
was broken
by the red gash of the salvia,
and the still open wound
of the pigeon's flight.

3

A palm squirrel
raced down a branch
of the mango tree
and disappeared
into the birdhouse.
She'd blocked
the entrance with fibre,
leaving an opening
for herself.
When she rushed out,
something pinkish fell
behind her.
It fell slowly, like a leaf.
On the ground I saw lying
a realistic animal toy.
It had four legs, a tail,
a thin pointed face.
Its eyes were closed.
It lay on its side.
I was still looking at it
when its pink skin quivered.
Next morning, the spot
where it fell was
covered with grass,
which had always been there.

4

She was sitting amidst trash
   under the iron wheelbarrow,
tugging at a bright green piece
   of linen cloth that kept getting
longer till she'd pulled it free.
   At first, she tried
to drag it as you would
   a palm frond. She dragged it
past a brick. Stopped. She
   dragged some more. Stopped.
She did a quick rethink and,
   one fold at a time, started
putting the cloth in her mouth
   till she had the whole thing
between her teeth with only
   the fringe showing. She did this
sitting on her hind legs.
   It was a long piece,
about the length of a necktie.
   Some of it would
slip out of her mouth
   as she ran. She'd then,
without stopping, stop
   and fold it back in. I saw her
entering a patch of tall
   grass where a tree stood,
her tree house somewhere in it.

5

A tailor bird hopped
near the water tank.
Were it not for the hop
I wouldn't have noticed.
Ahead of it was a cabbage white.
The few times the tailor bird
caught up with the butterfly,
it settled on the next leaf.
Neither was in a hurry.
Mornings tend to be still.
The night-flower's leaves
had been falling. I saw
the butterfly hobble.
The tailor bird had it in its beak
when it flew into the bougainvillea
from where it cheeped twice.
It sounded like a belch.
You couldn't have missed it.
I heard water trickling into
the water tank. Leaves fall
with their stalks attached.

IV

RESTING PLACES

1

That plop
  was the tailor bird's
hop as it left
  one branch
for the next, sending
  a ripple
through the tree.

2

I don't get
  this weather
where spring and fall
  happen together:

you can't see the ground
  for the leaves
nor the branches
  either.

3

Who says
  it is noiseless?
On the garden's
  turntable
it plays its web,
  moving
like a needle
  from edge
to centre.

Watching it,
  even birds
go silent.

4

A night wind and rattling windows.
In the morning, pine needles and
litchi blossoms sticking to wet earth.

The air is cool. The roof leaks.
It's due for repairs. The blossoms,
when I picked them, were light as ashes.

Found amidst garden refuse, a sapling.
Whether tree or shrub, in time, if the fruit's
edible, barbets will visit it.

5

A squirrel
jumped a marijuana.
It was the second attempt.

As the waist-high plant,
half bent, lay on the ground,
the squirrel

tore off a branch, stripped it
of leaves, held them
to its quivering mouth, ate.

The plant straightened itself
as if nothing had happened.
Nothing had.

6

Small as a newborn's fist,
birds travel towards the sky
as feathered arrows towards a receding

target, the deep blue turning pale
then paler, erasing birds,
fists, arrows, everything flung at it.

7

The purple sunbird
  comes and perches
at eye level
  on the iron ladder
and cheewits
  with a straight face
then does it again
  from a distance.
The purple of the king's mantle
  hums with bees.

8

Compared to others,
  the jungle babbler is
extra large. Size,

however, has nothing
  to do with it.
See it alighting

sideways on the tall
  stalk
of the Turk's turban,

bending it slightly.
  Birds will land
on their feet

as surely as the first
  drop of rain
will drive you inside.

9

Thunder and the sky grey.
  Bird chatter in trees.
Some of it in the silk oak.
  Being the tallest,
it's the first
  to catch the breeze
or lose a limb.
  The distant sound of rain
is now closer.

10

Bits of the canopy are missing.
There are holes in the foliage.
A branch's fallen over the telephone cable,
snapping it. The instrument was dead anyway.
Same time last year a neighbour lost a gulmohar.
Why can't I love her trees as I do my own?
We get bricklayers to raise walls
when an uncertain hedge will do.

11

The willow's been dead a long time.
It's a loose flagpole, a tall stump
that I can shake from side to side

with one hand. The king's mantle
entangled in its own profusion
has overrun it, though there's not much

for it to overrun.
The willow will fall when it will
and the forest floor do the rest.

12
En plein air

Through the cluster fig's
wide apart branches,

the dillenia, the curry leaf,
the mulberry, the Ceylon

ironwood and the forest of tall
self-seeded marijuana

each receives, equally
and together, the early

morning light.

13
Every morning I come here,
sit under the peach,
and water the eyes.

All around me, fanatical music plays.
As the fires get louder,
the smoke from it

makes the eyes smart.
There's never any rest
in resting places.

It's not the peach's fault.

14
I'm sitting in a less
    visited corner
of the garden.
    In front of me,
placed horizontally
    between two
mango trees,
    is a bamboo pole.
Like everything else,
    it's here for no reason.
Straight when it was
    cut, it sags
in the middle.
    A wide crack
runs along its length
    where ants move
as over a grey bridge.

15

Peering over the wall
  is a young boy
looking for his

basketball hidden under
  the bougainvillea; and trailing
on the ground

is a string that leads
  to a paper kite stuck
in the coral tree.

Not everything that
  comes into the garden
can be explained.

That leaf beside the metal
  folding chair I sit on,
unlike any leaf

I see around here,
  has the shape of a Japanese
hand fan.

I thought I'd take it inside
  and identify it
on Pl@ntNet.

Then it started to rain
  and the sun didn't come out
for two days.

16

Last night's rain
   water has collected
in the curled
   dillenia leaf
as in a brown
   bone-dry cup.

In it is reflected
   the curry plant
and the sky above.

　　　　*

On uneven stones
   bordering the flower bed,
examining the gaps
   between them,
a jungle babbler
   walks.

　　　　*

The risen sun
   is in my eyes,
and when I
   look at the trees
the leaves
   are black.

　　　　*

The pink
  periwinkle
is white
  underneath.

Fallen
  on the ground,
it's lying
  upside down.
How else
  would I know?

       *

Though it may not
know stealth,
the dark-winged fantail

as it flies over the mounds
of dead leaves,
changes its colour to fawn.

       *

All you need is a stake
  and a piece of twine,
though a pine needle
  will do just as well,
to prop up a wild petunia.

       *

What might
  the bird
be saying
  so loudly
so early
  in the morning?

17
Seen from the corner of my eye,
sitting a few feet from me,
what I thought was the brown street dog

that had again jumped over the gate
was a rhesus monkey scanning the trees, its baby
clinging to the fur as to slipping cloth.

18
Afraid I'll step on
  a young marigold,
if I walked to where I throw
  garden refuse

I stood under the stars
  flung the bitter melons
rotting in the fridge
  towards the mulberry.

19

Everything that dies
comes here: fronds
of the Chinese fan palm,
lopped or fallen branches,
sometimes an entire
hibiscus bush that had
mouldered at the base and was
still flowering. When it rains
the higgledy-piggledy will flatten.

There's no perimeter fence
to the gardens of the mind.
Unnoticed, clump by
clump, the mondo grass
extends its territory
and the bougainvillea that
collapsed under its own
weight in a storm is up
and spreading its thorns again.

20

In the earth
  lie their Gondi,
Swahili, or Latin
  roots. We see

only the bark,
  the leaf, or the fruit,
chewing on it
  every time we speak.

21

From its leaf
  leaf-plates are made
but I planted it
  for the red flower
that blooms in May.
  Despite its name,
the flame of the forest
  has never been lit.
The sun's late
  in rising. The breeze
touches a leaf,
  then touches another.
The sweetly singing
  magpie-robin's
been looking around.
  The one yesterday
found a dead gecko
  by the marigolds
and kept pecking at it
  till it saw blood.

22
Lady of the Night

I never went near it, not knowing
what it was called. A friend gave it
and I stuck it by a wall. Wrong spot.
It needed the sun. Then a bush
overran it and hid it from view
except for the flower

lowered like a long-fingered hand
trying out a bangle size. I never saw it
open. When it did, the scent, I'm told,
filled the garden and bats visited it.

23

After I came away,
I stood there
the longest time

watching the jungle babbler
perched on the bucket rim
drinking the water in it.

24

Rootless and headless,
   planted in a crack
in the skirting, the giloy
   is on its way up
the grille, one heart-shaped
   leaf at a time, each leaf
a footprint.

25

It rained overnight. The sun is out,
the light filtering through the trees
like clear water. It falls on the terracotta
birdbath, leaving some of it in shadow.
In the water, the dark shadows of leaves.

I walk to the end of the garden.
The two mangoes I spot lying on the ground
on the way back are raw and good for pickling.
A piece of the old house comes off in my hand.

26

Are the ants
taking away the earthworm
or is the earthworm moving
to shake off the ants?

It's too early for silverfish,
but there's one running
between the pages of the
notebook I write in.

27

The streetlight
    falling on them,
dead leaves
    look askance at

our love of adventure:
    climbing a jagged
stanza,
    equipped with a rope of sound.

28

Just the tail
  visible, sewn
into it
  with thread
and needle,
  it sits
on a branch
  like a puppet
on a string.
  Someone's
making
  the grey-green
bird
  sing upliftingly
in the tree.

29

They leave no leaf
  unturned, magpie-robin,
babbler and pigeon,
  as they gather
under the mulberry,
  as around a kitchen
table, looking for things
  to pick, forgetting
their squeaks, chirps,
  and *gutur-goo*s
for the moment.

30

When the monsoon rain fell
it left untouched the nest in the giloy
under the window ledge. I saw the fold
in the leaves before I did the red weaver ants
on the clothesline making their way to it.
The leaves were stitched one inside the other
with an opening at the top through which
the ants came and went. They then disappeared
into the pocket, leaving a few outside
to patrol the leaf surface night and day.
When after a week the leaves unfurled,
they had stretch marks on them
there was a dark stain on them like a birthmark
and were shrivelled around the edges.
There was no sign of the ants.

31

Knocked off the tree
   in a storm, this is where
it'll end, in a nest,
   still intact, holding
a stone palace,
   a victory tower, and
having room to spare.

32

The blue sky; the silk oak,
the birds in it playing to no audience.
They sound happy enough.

Then a door slams
and a motor starts.
Why are we here?

Why were we here at all?

V

A MATTER OF FACTS

Before the New Day

Before the new day issues new bills
in one-hour denominations and tells you how
to spend the small change, you look for the moment
that is not an alloy: the light not yet blue,
no cirrus clouds floating past in the sky
like fair swimmers in a pool, and the squirrels
yet to leave their nests. One pair lives
inside a birdhouse bought at a fair from a stall
selling woven rugs and wooden objects made
by local jailbirds. Some would be lifers.

Asleep in a Crib

Of sunlight on
the papaya grove
you have no memory.
Asleep in a crib,

unable to tell night from day,
one whitewashed wall from another,
a treepie's squawk
from the coppersmith's tap,

or river mouth from delta,
you'll reach the sea,
rising to nothingness
on your own silt.

Solstice

Lying on a camping cot under the peach,
I almost fall asleep. It's a winter morning.
There's much to do. I let the day slip.
I hear birds. Their calls mislead.
The ill-tempered treepie is sober feathered.
The preying kite sings most sweetly.
A rising empire doesn't see its end.
Night comes suddenly. The garden's quiet.
No one talks of the setting sun.

Brick Kiln

Somewhere are the short chimneys,
the moulds, the patch of earth
hollowed out to make your clay monument
whose pieces you stub your toe on
while you water the garden where

the wind doesn't stay on the leaf
nor the paradise flycatcher
in the tree, its long tail glimpsed
in thirds and fifths as it coils out
of the encircling green and is unsighted.

Rishikesh

It was there for a fluttering moment,
   knocking on the plate glass window
of the liveried hotel built with local
   limestone, the Himalayan flameback
with a red crest, a black and white
   checkered pattern on breast, a woodpecker bill
fashioned for drilling, before it returned
   to the sun-bearing clouds, the flattened
grey hills from whence it came.

Jay Walker

His head in the air,
his nose to the ground,
like a kite in the sky he freely
roams on fixed wings and knows
all manner of earthly things,
like the name of each hillock
in a hilly district and the year
it was made to disappear.

A Matter of Facts

1

When the bottlebrush in the park
saw her walking backwards, doing her
fifty steps, it stopped dropping
its red spikes and moved aside.

Just then, a one-legged man
who'd turned a broomstick without a broom
into a flagpole with a tricolour, flew
across the street with his possessions.

It was the day after Independence Day.
I didn't see any sparrows today.
It's not that my eyes are weak.
It's just that there are no sparrows.

2

I thought the black butterfly
with yellow polka dots
was a bow tie the squirrel had
clipped on. Dodging the other squirrels,
it disappeared into a bush. Last seen,
it was running up the far side
of the Java plum with its dinner.

Another day, a feral cat's tail
curled out from under the amaranth plants.
I couldn't see its prey. The dillenia leaves

made a dry sound when it walked through them
noiselessly. It was a young cat, taking
hunting lessons from its mother,
who then chased it through the leaves.

3

It's only now that night has fallen does the wind
reach me under the trees where, bringing the chair out
and choosing a spot for it, the same one I always do,
I've waited since morning. Twirling its ribbons,
the paradise flycatcher somersaults through the air,
and the ribbonless female comes and sits
on the birdbath's rim. She looks around, makes sure
that no one's looking, and jumps in. Droplets pop
like flashbulbs when she steps out into the sun
and shakes herself dry. The ungainly grey hornbill
arrives for its first meal, scattering more mulberries
than it eats, staining the ground purple. I fold the chair
and bring it inside. The fruitless day has ended well.

Sparrow Population

Earlier I'd hear them
in garden bushes

or, rising as one, saw them
scatter like a handful

of grain. Surely
they could not all

have been killed
before a festival crowd

of witnesses
for crossing the street

to be with their lovers.
Some were found dead

beside spotless railway tracks,
or hanging from the same branch

of unfrequented trees, the leaves
aglow in the last light.

The air hums.
There's a beat of wings.

Sparrow souls have made
their home there.

Yesterday,
on the veranda floor,

I saw a young scorpion
and slippered it to death.

New Turmeric Leaf

I sneeze.
Sneezes don't come
singly. My eyes,
when I open them,
feel wet, the trees
blurry. The nose too
is wet. I look for my
handkerchief.

When I settle down again,
before me, piercing
the ground like a
stiletto, I see the upthrust
of a new turmeric leaf.

Torso

Headless, the arms missing, like a torso
in the Roman gallery, was the dead tree.
The leaves from other trees kept falling.
A young boy, his chin resting on his hands
resting on the park railing, was looking at them.

Forever the lives that go on around us.
You spot a brown butterfly with orange
wingtips. It disappears. What disappears
is its own monument, like a lightning bolt
that strikes unseen after it has passed.

Three or Four Squirrels,
Two Bulbuls, One Magpie-Robin

A squirrel ran for its life.
It crossed a flower bed and stopped.
Its pursuer lost interest.
Afterwards, I saw them
running round the Java plum.
They're pests and they all
look the same. Unlike birds,
only squirrels know
why they do certain things.
Why they raise themselves
on their hind legs to reach
the tops of inedible plants
or why they deflower
young marigolds. The older
of the two bulbuls
awaited its turn at the birdbath.
The younger one stood on the rim,
looking around, looking
at the magpie-robin
opposite it. As soon as the robin
got off the rim, the bulbul
dipped its beak into the water.
How much water does a beak
hold? The older bulbul
walked up to the birdbath
after the other two had left.
They're both species of least concern.

No sooner had the rain

No sooner had the rain stopped
than the babblers were out.
How did they know it had stopped?
They too had been watching the sky
through the leaves.

They sat on a stone,
one of several edging the flowerbed,
and from there, one behind the other,
walked to the marijuana patch,
studying the ground with their beaks.
They must still get grit with the seed.

They sat on a barbed wire.
Next, they were on the mango tree
in the neighbour's garden.
Above me, a leaf shook.
It was a raindrop.
A raindrop isn't nothing.

Ants

Early morning
a riderless horse
galloped

down the road,
behind it
came the horseless rider.

They met up ahead
and galloped past me again
as I went past

a slow-moving man,
his eyes fixed
to the ground,

a paper bag in his hand,
who stopped every few yards
to sprinkle flour

on a nest of ants.
Like the horse,
like the rider,

like me,
like the slow-moving man,
the ants were restless.

Avenue Tree in Private Garden

Hidden by the dillenia,
from a certain angle by the ironwood,
and overshadowed by the cluster fig,
is the laburnum seeking the sky above it.
In hottest summer, shining like common
living room lights, it would have
chandeliers of bright yellow flowers. Today
I noticed the trunk had bald white patches.

From one of them a new branch stuck out.
The branch above it was bone dry. I heard
a koel and was distracted. It stopped
mid-sentence then resumed the call. From
the corner of my eye I heard the tailor bird.
It sounded like a packet of needles.
The koel's call rose above it, much like
the cluster fig's canopy over the laburnum.

A tree lives till it falls, and even then.

Parasite

No flowers that would've given it away,
its root soldered to a branch of the silk oak,
it was going to take over the tree had not

an old Gurjar, hard up, seeking work,
recognized the parasitical growth
from the street and propelled by his hands

and bare feet, the machete his sole
accessory, shimmied up the trunk and
lopped off the host branch. Wherever it went next,

carried by wind, bird, or however plants travel,
I was sad to see it go, happy to have
the Gurjar back on safe ground.

When the parasite returns, he'll come round again.

Hack

I cannot face the mango tree
Yesterday I had it amputated
On a whim

The branch extended like an arm over the garden
There were blossoms at its fingertips
This is springtime

For years it had shielded me
From the ruckus within myself
I'm now left alone to face the music

Fire Wall

They grow like plants,
the kitchen walls.
You pull one out,
another takes root
in soil rich with black
manure, the peelings
of the unswept floor.

Of copper, iron, and
stainless steel, tropical
vessels dully shine
on trees, as the decades
play out. The oven's on
high, sometimes on low.
It's never on off.

Registry of Births, Deaths and Marriages

1   The Crouch

A fetal
crouch.

Not that the Wiki stub
expanded

will still give
your mother's

name. All the same,
as you stretched,

jogged, or
practiced

yogic breathing
or stood on one leg

and counted to
ten slowly

a squirrel
hopped

out of sight,
as have you.

Ouch!

II   The Mill

We come
of mixed grain.
Newly threshed,

some locally
sourced,
fed into the mill,

we are
what's poured back
into it again.

The mill
is made
by Favre-Leuba.

Possibly Theban

A young curly haired
man, possibly Theban, looks
at you with wide open eyes
as you enter the room.

He removes the panel,
the mummy wrappings,
and unnoticed
by the museum staff

walks towards the street
where a visitor
has got off the bus
to take his place

in the sarcophagus. Few
of the Sunday crowd
stop to read the caption.
It hasn't changed,

nor has the display.

Cremation at Nalapani Road

As I absently watched the four ashen
joss sticks on the stone platform flicker and die,
my mother's face flickered and died so quickly
that I almost didn't notice the flicker.
Nothing burns out till everything burns out.
I still leave the light on in her room
and wait for dawn to flood the dark stairwell.

Approaching 80

At 20, meeting an 80-year-old,
I'd wonder what it's like
to be 80. Now I know.
It's like being 20 again,
except that along the way

fathers have breakdowns,
mothers dementia,
family houses are sold,
and young men arm wrestle
in the park, as their friends

look on cheeringly.

Nothing Worked Out
Suryakant Tripathi 'Nirala'

Nothing worked out, and so what?
The gods betrayed us. Do we weep over it?

Everywhere, shadows and more shadows,
yet they showed blue sky.
You become less and become more,
you go away and you return.
When nothing could've happened,
what could've happened?
So, nothing worked out, and so what?

You walk, and grow weary,
you stop, and you whine.
It's the world's fault.
What can one say?
What's been washed clean,
why scrub it again?
Nothing worked out, and so what?

Translated from Hindi

We'll Never Know the Names

We'll never know the names of the trees
buried in this property through which a lane
with two blind turns now passes. Fortified viewy
houses on either side and always
room for one more. Behind a disappearing
stack of bricks, men raise a wall.

In broad strips, light funnels through the branches
of the cluster fig. The buttress roots are new.
The original trees the summer storms
left untouched have long since been felled,
forgotten by the struggling birds,
the parcelled earth on which they stood, the wind.

Occasionally, when it found
an undisturbed spot beside a garage or shed,
a seed, like love, took root and became a tree again
that marauding boys climbed for the fruit,
though none knew where the seed was from and if
the tree was planted or had come up on its own.

House of Peeling Walls

I leave this house to the birds in the birdbath
To the leaves that float down like feathers from the sky
To the Lakhori brick I hold in my hand
To the black ants that live inside the walls
To their ears that hear thunder before there's thunder to be heard
To the irises that climb over stones when they get in the way
To the shingles that came down rivers when there were rivers
To the flowering clover that spreads like fire
To the buttress root that uprooted the garden shed
To the dawn that widens the crack in its roof when light seeps in
To the bougainvillea twigs thorning the ground I step on
To the woodpile stacked against a leaning wall
To the new leaves of March that arrive with a cracker burst
To the rose vine that doesn't know where to stop
To the water in the iron bucket
To the squirrel that darts round the corner
                                    of a medium-sized country

Like a Stone

To be still
like a stone
a rock formation
or a hill

To find
one's cadence
where one
is

Aubade

1

Each dawn that breaks
is one dawn less.
More's the reason
to keep returning
from dawn to sunset
to the pull of the hard lead,

the starkness of paper,
the glistening point
that rubs and strokes
and leaves
an overwhelming stain
on the white sheet.

2

By the time I put
lead in the pencil,
the words were lost.
They'll come back,
not that they ever have.

They had something to do
with dying, with holding
the fullness of dawn in one's beak
and around one's feathers.

VI

SMALL HOLDINGS

1

A mason's trowel raised it.
Sledgehammer and crowbar brought it down.
The cluster fig's buttress roots

pried loose a wall. Rising damp
discoloured the chequerboard floor.
There was a lot of dust.

Stacked by the garden shed
are Lakhori bricks from the veranda.
Your parents, newly wed,

had posed under its arch.
You can only return to the house you live in
by crawling back the way you came.

2

Though you keep returning to the places
you never left, heirlooms will sink
to the bottom of risen seas. Hold on
to what you have as buttress roots do
to the wild patch of sunlight even as
the sun shifts to the hedge struggling under it
and thence to the hail-damaged taro leaf
before it goes over the watchtowered wall
that no man can scale, much less the family silver.

3
Let the lopped branch
of the Java plum
caught in the peach
stay where it is.

The squirrel uses
the shortcut, as if
it had always been there,
to reach the crepe myrtle.

4
The sun rises
and night flips the page
of the pop-up book.

There are no readers
for the title
but it stays in print.

On its cover,
a tree, unrisen
from the ground.

5
Except for bird noises,
mornings have the stillness
of hanging fruit, not that the mud apple
has borne any. Dwarfed by its neighbours,

it's now catching up. The garden's never still.
Wearing cushion cover stripes, the common
glider sails by, and the magpie-robin
comes to the gate for a quick look.

6

Like everything else, the thorny
asparagus fern takes root wherever
and follows the first trail it sees.

The one under the frangipani
spreads along its dependable branches.
Another attaches itself to the climbing rose,

and now you cannot separate the two.

7

As you wait for dawn
and see the warm light
of the desk lamp reflected
in the window glass,

you know it's time to remove
the books from the bookcase,
the polish from the wood,
and read the exposed grain.

8

At a 60-degree angle,
the lemon tree beside the shady Java plum
leans towards the house, seeking light.
The fruit's turning yellow. You sit
where you always do, today

facing the birdbath. It's unoccupied.
The short-eared owl comes for a dip.
Without looking around, he goes straight in.
Your eyes meet before he leaves.
The morning doesn't leave you alone.

9

There are mornings when
there's no wind.
The bitter melon shrivels
on the vine and the lemon tree's
capsized leaves fill the birdbath.

When everything seems to be over,
at a distance of a few feet,
tiny marijuana plants appear
like a crowd on the horizon
rushing towards you.

10

A feral cat has made the veranda chair
her home. She climbs over a pair of sneakers
and goes out, keeping an eye on her kittens.

One of them was run over in the lane,
its small head unaffected. With the first rains,
woodfern and amaranth arrive like claimants
at the doorstep. There's a low wall,
its bricks pried loose by the undergrowth.
Every monsoon it leans a little more,
the new leaves unfurling like hoisted flags.

11

Despite its chimney-like height,
before the Java plum can
turn a leaf to catch the drift,

the nasturtium shows up
to register the wind
you watch slip by.

Dip your hand in the stream,
and every once in a while
test the current on your skin.

There's little else to do.

12

Squirrels are small eaters.
If one finds a crumb, the others
go about their business or,
chased away, return later.
None go empty handed.

With a turn of the head
the scenery changes.
His hand inside his sleeve,
last year's scarecrow
waves to this year's birds,

and there's a piece of bangle glass
on the ground.
Take your eyes off it and you won't
find it again. It's happened before.
You've lost a needle in a drawer.

13
It's all you can give them –
a bit of trodden earth,
and thin, pebbly soil.

They come up all the same,
eager, green, abundant –
amaranth, sesame, basil.